at blanchard's table

at blanchard's table

A Trip to the Beach Cookbook

Melinda Blanchard and Robert Blanchard

Authors of

A Trip to the Beach

Photographs by Ben Fink

With additional photographs by Wyatt Counts

Clarkson Potter/Publishers
New York

This book is dedicated to

Lowell, Clinton, Miguel, Bug, Alwyn, Garrilin, Rinso, Hughes,

Alex, Ozzie, Tarah, Carlos, and Wayne—all of whom make up

the extraordinary family at Blanchard's Restaurant.

Text copyright © 2003 by Melinda Blanchard and Robert Blanchard
All color photographs except as noted by Ben Fink. Color photographs on pages 10, 11, 61, and 79 by Wyatt Counts. All black-and-white photographs except as noted by Wyatt Counts. Black-and-white photographs on pages 24, 148, 156, 164, 165, 169, 172, 176, 181, 185, and 205 are by Ben Fink. Photograph on page 45 by Melinda Blanchard.

Published by Clarkson Potter/Publishers, New York, New York. Member of the Crown Publishing Group, a division of Random House, Inc.
www.randomhouse.com

CLARKSON N. POTTER is a trademark and POTTER and colophon are registered trademarks of Random House, Inc.

Printed in Singapore

Design by Maggie Hinders

Library of Congress Cataloging-in-Publication Data
Blanchard, Melinda
    At Blanchard's table: a trip to the beach cookbook
Melinda Blanchard and Robert Blanchard.
        p.   cm.
1. Cookery.   I. Blanchard, Melinda   II. Title.
TX714 .B5748   2003
641.5—dc21   2002004432

ISBN 0-609-61082-1

10 9 8 7 6 5 4 3 2 1

First Edition

Acknowledgments

Many people helped create this book and we are sincerely grateful to them all.

Michael Carlisle is our cherished friend, agent, and mentor. His encouragement allows us to follow our dreams, and for that we love him more than he knows.

We are deeply grateful to our editor, Annetta Hanna, who continually gives us the confidence to transport readers to Anguilla and Vermont. Many thanks to all of our friends at Clarkson Potter and Crown Publishing whose attention to every detail makes them the best in the business: Pam Krauss, Lauren Shakely, Marysarah Quinn, Leigh Ann Ambrosi, Elizabeth Royles, Jean Lynch, Maggie Hinders, Ronnie Grinberg, Linnea Knollmueller, and everyone else behind the scenes, including copyeditor Jude Grant. We thank you all from the bottom of our hearts.

Many photo props were generously loaned to us by friends and we thank you all: Betsy Siebeck and Gary Smith, C. Beston & Company, Bob and Nancy Bean, and our friends at Main Street Kitchens. And a big thanks to Jane and Jim Harmon for constant support and encouragement.

Special thanks to our friends and neighbors in Vermont for helping with recipe ideas as well as tasting whenever needed: Marty James, Deb Van Armen, Alan and Becky Joffrey, Pat Merrill, and the gang at the Hitchcock payroll office.

And as always, love and thanks to Jesse and Maggie whose exceptional palates help fine-tune our recipes both for this book as well as the restaurant. We'll keep testing as long as you keep tasting.

Contents

at
blanchard's
table

Introduction

When Blanchard's Restaurant first opened, everyone asked what kind of food we served. The question terrified Melinda. What they expected was a clear, descriptive label. Something they could identify with. Was it Caribbean, Mediterranean, Asian, French, Italian? She had no intelligible answer and offered one bumbling response after another. Now, after nine years of practice, the lack of a single-word description still makes her uncomfortable.

Casual Starters

* Antipasto Dip
* In a Hurry

    Prosciutto Bundles ∎ Balsamic Goat Cheese ∎ White Bean Puree with Bacon ∎ Easy Antipasto ∎ Chutney and Cheese ∎ Asparagus Wrapped in Smoked Salmon

* Feta Cheese Spread with Herbs and Garlic
* Herbed Goat Cheese Dip
* Green Peppercorn Dip
* Blanchard's Lobster Cakes with Tomato Tartar Sauce
* Hot Artichoke Dip with Shrimp, Mustard, and Mozzarella
* Baguette Stuffed with Sun-Dried Tomatoes, Mascarpone, and Basil
* Roquefort Dip
* Smoked Salmon Spread
* Prosciutto-Wrapped Lemon Chicken with Avocado and Lime Dip
* Crusty Grilled Shrimp with Soy-Sesame Sauce
* Grilled Bread with Three Toppings: Sweet-and-Sour Peppers ∎ Roasted Cherry Tomatoes, Fresh Mozzarella, and Spinach ∎ Sun-Dried Tomato Puree with Shiitake Mushrooms
* Marinated Ginger Shrimp with Lemon-Parmesan Dipping Sauce
* Hummus with an Extra Burst of Lemon

Antipasto Dip

* MAKES 2 CUPS

USE ANY LEFTOVERS OF THIS FLAVORFUL DIP TO SPOON ONTO BAKED
POTATOES. ■ MAKE SURE YOU DON'T PUREE THE VEGETABLES—IT'S
MUCH BETTER IF YOU BITE INTO THE LITTLE CHUNKS OF FLAVOR.

8 ounces	cream cheese, at room temperature
¾ cup	sour cream
¼ cup	Hellmann's mayonnaise
10	kalamata olives, pitted, drained and chopped
2	canned artichoke bottoms, drained and chopped
10	sun-dried tomatoes packed in oil, drained, and chopped
2	scallions (white and green parts), thinly sliced
1 teaspoon	salt
1 teaspoon	freshly ground black pepper

Combine the cream cheese, sour cream, and mayonnaise in a food processor and puree until well blended. Add the olives, artichokes, sun-dried
tomatoes, scallions, salt, and pepper. Pulse several times to mix. The dip
should remain slightly chunky with visible bits of olives, tomatoes, and scallions. Serve chilled or at room temperature.

HAVE YOU EVER bought a can of
artichoke bottoms? Not hearts, but
bottoms. For some reason, hearts
are more widely used but the
bottoms have much more artichoke
flavor. Try sautéing them with a
little olive oil and garlic to spoon
over grilled chicken or seafood, or
just cut them into quarters and add
to pasta and salads.

In a Hurry

Prosciutto Bundles

Wrap a small piece of prosciutto around raw shrimp, scallops, or canned, drained whole water chestnuts. Secure each with a toothpick that has been soaked in water for 30 minutes. Grill or broil until cooked through. Serve with mustard or your favorite dip or creamy salad dressing. (Bacon is a good substitute for the prosciutto, if you prefer.)

Balsamic Goat Cheese

Blend ½ pound of goat cheese with 1 tablespoon of balsamic vinegar and a generous grinding of black pepper. Garnish with chopped chives and serve with slices of sourdough bread or assorted crackers.

White Bean Puree with Bacon

Place 1 can of drained cannellini beans in a food processor with a teaspoon or so of lemon juice. Puree the beans, adding a little water as needed to make a smooth, creamy mixture. Transfer to a medium mixing bowl and stir in a generous handful of crumbled, cooked bacon, plenty of chopped black olives, and a sprinkling of thyme. Season with salt and pepper, garnish with chopped parsley, and serve with crackers or crudités.

Easy Antipasto

An oversized platter filled with an assortment of meats and vegetables makes an impressive and quick antipasto to serve with cocktails. In 10 minutes, you can assemble a variety of colors, shapes, and flavors and be ready to join the party. Use your imagination. A few suggestions: roasted red bell peppers (from a jar), whole caper berries with stems, assorted olives, sliced hard salami, Parmesan cheese cut into small wedges or shaved with a vegetable peeler, and prosciutto wrapped around chunks of fresh mozzarella.

Chutney and Cheese

Blend some of your favorite chutney with softened cream cheese for a speedy dip. Don't worry about exactly how much chutney to use—just add enough to make the cream cheese the right consistency for dipping. Add a dash of Worcestershire sauce for extra zing.

Asparagus Wrapped in Smoked Salmon

Wrap slices of smoked salmon around stalks of blanched, chilled asparagus. Top with a few grindings of black pepper and chill before serving.

Blanchard's Lobster Cakes with Tomato Tartar Sauce
✳ MAKES ABOUT THIRTY 2-INCH CAKES

IF BLANCHARD'S RESTAURANT HAS A SIGNATURE DISH, THIS IS IT. WHEN CUSTOMERS WERE INVITED TO ONE OF OUR SON'S ART OPENINGS IN NEW YORK, THEY SAID THEY WOULD ONLY COME IF WE MADE LOBSTER CAKES. (WE WEREN'T REALLY SURE IF THEY WERE JOKING OR NOT, SO WE MADE THEM JUST IN CASE.) AND WHEN PEOPLE HEARD WE WERE WRITING A COOKBOOK, THE FIRST QUESTION WAS WHETHER OR NOT THIS RECIPE WOULD BE INCLUDED. HERE IT IS. ENJOY!

3 tablespoons	unsalted butter
¾ cup	all-purpose flour
2 cups	milk
1 pound	cooked lobster meat, coarsely chopped and patted dry
1½ cups	red bell pepper, diced small and patted dry
¼ cup	scallions (white and green parts), thinly sliced
½ teaspoon	cayenne pepper
¾ teaspoon	salt
½ tablespoon	freshly ground black pepper
1½ cups	fresh bread crumbs
	Equal amounts of butter and olive oil, for sautéing
1 to 1½ cups	Tomato Tartar Sauce (recipe follows)

In a large, deep-sided saucepan, heat the butter over a low heat until it stops foaming. Add the flour gradually and cook for 2 minutes, whisking continually. Add the milk ½ cup at a time, whisking constantly to get rid of the lumps. Simmer for 5 minutes, continuing to whisk until thick and smooth. Remove from the heat and set aside.

In a large bowl, combine the lobster, peppers, scallions, cayenne, salt, and pepper. Add 1 cup of the bread crumbs and the milk mixture, and mix well. Cool to room temperature. Shape into small 1- to 1½-inch balls and flatten slightly. The lobster cakes should be about ½ inch thick. Coat the cakes with more bread crumbs.

Heat a layer of butter and oil in a sauté pan over medium heat until hot but not smoking. Cook the lobster cakes until golden brown on both sides. Drain on paper towels and serve hot with Tomato Tartar Sauce.

N O T E : As an alternative, cooked shrimp or crab can be substituted for the lobster.

casual starters casual starters casual starters casual starters casual starters casual starters casual starters casual starters casual starters casual starters casual starte

23

Baguette Stuffed with Sun-Dried Tomatoes, Mascarpone, and Basil

✴ SERVES 6 TO 8

IF YOU'RE LOOKING FOR A 10-MINUTE RECIPE TO SERVE AT A PARTY, HERE IT IS. GIVE IT A FEW SPINS IN THE FOOD PROCESSOR, SPREAD THE MIXTURE INTO A HOLLOWED-OUT BAGUETTE, AND SLICE. YOU CAN SUBSTITUTE ANY SPREAD AND USE THE SAME METHOD, BUT CHOOSE ONE WITH A BIT OF COLOR SO IT SHOWS UP AGAINST THE BREAD.

1½ cups	sun-dried tomatoes packed in oil, drained
12 ounces	mascarpone cheese
¼ cup	coarsely chopped fresh basil
1 teaspoon	coarsely chopped fresh mint
1 teaspoon	salt
½ teaspoon	freshly ground black pepper
1	baguette
	Fresh basil, for garnish

Coarsely chop the sun-dried tomatoes in a food processor. Add the mascarpone and pulse until mixed but not pureed. There should still be bits of tomato visible. Add the basil, mint, salt, and pepper, and pulse until just mixed. Do not puree.

Cut the baguette in half lengthwise and use a spoon to scrape out most of the inside of the bread. Fill both sides of the baguette with the mixture and put the halves back together to form a whole loaf again. Slice the filled baguette on an angle into ½-inch-thick rounds. Serve at room temperature on a platter lined with large, fresh basil leaves.

N O T E : Skip the bread and just fill a bowl with this delicious sun-dried tomato mixture. Serve as a spread with crackers.

blanchard's table at blanchard's table at blanchard's table at blanchard's table at blanchard's table at blanchard's table at blanchard's table at blanchard's table at blanchard's tab

26

Prosciutto-Wrapped Lemon Chicken with Avocado and Lime Dip

✳ MAKES ABOUT 20 PIECES

THE CHICKEN HERE HAS TO MARINATE FOR 1 TO 2 HOURS, SO MAKE SURE TO GIVE YOURSELF ENOUGH TIME. ALTHOUGH IT TAKES A LITTLE EFFORT, THIS RECIPE IS NOT DIFFICULT AND WELL WORTH IT. THE TARTNESS OF THE LEMON AND THE CRISPY STRIPS OF SAVORY PROSCIUTTO MAKE A DELICIOUS COMBINATION. IT'S A BLANCHARD'S RESTAURANT CLASSIC. SERVE WARM WITH THE AVOCADO AND LIME DIP.

1 pound	boneless, skinless chicken breast halves
½ cup	olive oil
½ cup	freshly squeezed lemon juice
2 teaspoons	Worcestershire sauce
½ teaspoon	salt
½ teaspoon	freshly ground black pepper
12 thin slices	prosciutto
20	whole fresh basil leaves
1 cup	Avocado and Lime Dip (recipe follows)

Cut the chicken into ½-inch-thick strips that are 3 inches long and ½ inch wide. Combine the oil, lemon juice, Worcestershire sauce, salt, and pepper in a medium bowl. Add the chicken and marinate in the refrigerator for 1 to 2 hours.

Prepare the grill or preheat the broiler.

Place a slice of the prosciutto on a cutting board. Cut in half crosswise to make two pieces approximately 5 inches long. Place a whole basil leaf on the top piece of the prosciutto and put a strip of chicken on the basil. Roll the prosciutto and basil around the chicken to form a 3-inch cylinder. Repeat the process until all the chicken strips are rolled. Grill or broil the bundles just until the chicken is firm and cooked through, about 5 minutes. Serve immediately.

al starters casual starters casual starters casual starters casual starters casual starters casual starters casual starters casual starters casual starters casual starter

31

Sun-Dried Tomato Puree with Shiitake Mushrooms

✳ SERVES 6

HERE'S ANOTHER VERSATILE RECIPE THAT WELCOMES CREATIVE USES.
WE'VE SERVED THESE MUSHROOMS ON TOP OF SWORDFISH, TOSSED
THEM WITH PASTA, AND SPOONED THEM OVER MASHED POTATOES.

1 cup	sun-dried tomatoes packed in oil, drained
¼ cup	balsamic vinegar
⅓ cup plus ½ cup	olive oil
	Salt and freshly ground black pepper
2 medium	garlic cloves, minced
1 pound	shiitake mushroom caps, sliced ¼ inch thick
3 tablespoons	fresh thyme leaves or 1½ tablespoons dried
1 loaf	hearty, rustic bread, sliced ½ inch thick

Puree the tomatoes, vinegar, and ⅓ cup of the oil in a food processor. With the machine running, add a little water as necessary to make the puree the consistency of a thick ketchup. Taste for salt and pepper, and set aside.

In a large sauté pan, heat 3 tablespoons of the oil over medium heat. Add the garlic and mushrooms, and cook until the mushrooms are tender and no liquid remains in the pan. Remove from the heat. Add the thyme and taste for salt and pepper.

Grill or toast both sides of the bread until golden brown. Drizzle with the remaining oil (should be about ⅓ cup) and spread with a generous amount of the tomato puree. Spoon the mushrooms on top of the puree and serve immediately.

No Help Wanted

ASK ANY RESTAURATEUR IN THE UNITED STATES to describe his single biggest headache, and without hesitation the most common answer will be staffing. We have a friend in the business who struggles so much that he runs frequent newspaper ads offering $500 hiring bonuses in an effort to recruit new employees. The truth is that other than management, restaurant employees are typically just passing through on their way to what they call a *real* job. This transient nature of wait staff, prep cooks, and dishwashers makes for a challenging work environment, to say the least.

The good food and romance found at Blanchard's Restaurant is created not by people who trudge to work wishing they were somewhere else. Quite the opposite. Our staff is our greatest joy. We have thirteen sincere, job-loving people, most of whom have been with us from the start. They consider Blanchard's their home and take pleasure in doing whatever it takes to make guests happy.

Job descriptions at Blanchard's are much fuzzier than at other restaurants. For instance, Miguel, our wine steward, can be found snipping pink bougainvillea out in the garden before dinner. He sits at the bar before the first guests arrive and carefully arranges the flowers in tiny bud vases for each table. His pride in perfecting every detail is evident. Now just try asking a wine steward in New York to arrange flowers before dinner each night!

Lowell, our restaurant manager, works in the kitchen every morning with sous-chef Clinton, simmering sauces and blending salad dressings. And Clinton, in turn, helps fix a leaky roof or paint a garden bench whenever needed. There are no boundaries of duties and responsibilities. Everyone is working toward the same goal.

People ask us how we cope with hurricanes and the frustration of having to fly in all of our food and supplies. The answer is that we're not facing those problems alone. After a storm our staff shows up with hammers and saws ready to rebuild and start again. And when the baby lettuce is wilting at customs, it's Lowell and Miguel who scurry around to speed up the process.

When we moved to Anguilla, the benefits of sun, sand, and palm trees were obvious. But our staff turned out to be the biggest benefit of all. Cheers to life's extraordinary surprises!

Soups

* Chunky Gazpacho
* Vermont Cheddar Soup
* Blanchard's Corn Chowder
* All-Year-Long Tomato Soup with Carrots, Spinach, and Asiago Cheese
* Three-Mushroom Soup
* Chilled Avocado-Lime Soup with Shrimp and Chilies
* Spicy Coconut and Sweet Potato Soup
* Easy Vegetable, Bean, and Macaroni Soup

Blanchard's Corn Chowder

* SERVES 8

THE WORD *CHOWDER* CONJURES UP THOUGHTS OF SOUPS
THICKENED WITH RICH, HEAVY CREAM. THIS CHOWDER INSTEAD
GETS ITS BODY FROM PUREED VEGETABLES. IT'S LIGHTER, FRESHER,
AND PACKED WITH FLAVOR.

3 tablespoons	unsalted butter
3	medium yellow onions, chopped
5	carrots, cut into ¼-inch slices
5	celery stalks, cut into ¼-inch slices
6 cups	fresh corn kernels (about 12 ears of corn)
3 cups	chicken broth
¾ teaspoon	salt
½ teaspoon	freshly ground black pepper
2	large red bell peppers, seeded and cut into ½-inch pieces
3 tablespoons	chopped fresh dill, plus more for garnish

Melt the butter in a large pot. When the butter is hot, add the onion,
carrots, and celery and cook just until tender, stirring frequently, 10 to
12 minutes. Add the corn and cook 2 minutes more. Remove 4 cups of the
vegetables and transfer to a food processor. Puree the mixture until fairly
smooth and return it to the soup pot.

Add the chicken broth, salt, and pepper, and bring to a boil. As soon as
it boils, add the peppers and simmer for 2 minutes. Add the dill, and taste
for salt and pepper. Serve hot, garnished with more dill.

soups soups

47

Salads and Dressings

* Grilled Corn and Chicken Salad
* In a Hurry
     Please Toss the Greens ■ Crispy Prosciutto ■ Asian Cucumber Salad ■
     Beets in the Raw ■ Marinated Shiitakes and Spinach ■ Sushi Tomatoes
* Grilled Steak and Onion Salad
* Chicken Salad with Peas, Peppers, and Hummus Dressing
* Chicken and Green Bean Salad with Kalamata Olive Dressing
* Telephone Cord Fusilli with Vegetables and Sesame Dressing
* Lemon Shrimp Salad with Asian Greens and Bean Thread Noodles
* Potato Salad with Lime and Sun-Dried Tomatoes
* Asparagus with Mustard and Thyme
* Grilled Portobello Mushrooms Stacked with Spinach and Shaved Parmesan
* Caesar Salad with Homemade Parmesan Croutons
* Roasted Beet Salad with Cranberry Vinaigrette and Blue Cheese
* Black Bean Salad with Couscous, Peppers, and Peas
* Orzo Salad with Corn, Tomatoes, Feta, and Chili-Lime Vinaigrette
* Spicy Vegetable Slaw
* Additional Dressings ■ Lemon-Pepper Vinaigrette ■ Whole-Grained
  Mustard and Lemon Dressing ■ Balsamic Vinaigrette ■ Parmesan-Pepper
  Dressing ■ Homemade Ranch Dressing ■ Rice Wine Vinaigrette with
  Ginger ■ Blue Cheese Vinaigrette

Grilled Steak and Onion Salad

✳ SERVES 6

WE'VE EATEN SEARED STEAK PILED HIGH WITH SAUTÉED ONIONS IN STEAK HOUSES FOR YEARS. THIS SALAD IS A VARIATION ON THAT THEME AND A DELICIOUS SUMMERTIME ALTERNATIVE. IT MAKES A GREAT SEASIDE PICNIC IN ANGUILLA AND IS JUST AS MUCH AT HOME ON OUR PORCH IN VERMONT.

⅓ cup	rice wine vinegar
1	garlic clove, minced
1½ tablespoons	minced peeled fresh ginger
1 tablespoon	soy sauce
¼ cup	sherry
3 tablespoons	hoisin sauce
1 teaspoon	Dijon mustard
2 tablespoons	olive oil
4	large yellow onions, sliced ½ inch thick
2	yellow bell peppers, seeded and cut into 2-inch-wide strips
	Vegetable oil, for basting
	Salt and freshly ground black pepper
2	New York strip steaks (12 ounces each)
4 to 5 cups	torn pieces of lettuce

Prepare the grill.

Make the dressing while the grill is heating: In a small bowl, whisk together the vinegar, garlic, ginger, soy sauce, sherry, hoisin, mustard, and olive oil. Set aside.

Brush the onion slices and yellow peppers with vegetable oil and season with salt and pepper. Grill the vegetables slowly over medium heat until soft and slightly charred, about 10 minutes. Take them off the grill and separate the onion slices into rings. Grill the steak until desired doneness, about 6 minutes on each side for medium. Cut the steak against the grain into ¼-inch slices.

Toss the greens with a very light coating of dressing and arrange on a serving platter or individual plates. Spread the onions and peppers on top of the lettuce and arrange the sliced steak attractively on top, allowing the onions and peppers to show through. Drizzle a little more dressing over the salad and serve warm.

blanchard's table at blanchard's table at blanchard's table at blanchard's table at blanchard's table at blanchard's table at blanchard's table at blanchard's table

58

Chicken and Green Bean Salad with Kalamata Olive Dressing

✳ SERVES 6

WHEN WE DELIVERED A SAMPLING OF FIVE CHICKEN SALADS TO OUR FRIENDS AND NEIGHBORS FOR REVIEWS, THIS WAS THE UNANIMOUS WINNER.

3 pounds	boneless, skinless chicken breast halves
2 to 3 cups	chicken broth
1¼ pounds	green beans, preferably haricots verts, trimmed
⅓ cup	pitted kalamata olives
1 tablespoon	Dijon mustard
2 teaspoons	freshly grated lemon peel
1	garlic clove, minced
2 tablespoons	freshly squeezed lemon juice
2 teaspoons	anchovy paste
⅓ cup	olive oil
¾ teaspoon	salt
½ teaspoon	freshly ground black pepper
	Green leaf lettuce, for serving
12	cherry tomatoes, quartered

Preheat the oven to 350°F.

Arrange the chicken in a single layer in a shallow baking pan and pour in enough broth to cover. Cover the pan with foil and bake until done, about 30 minutes. Remove from the oven, let the chicken cool in the broth to room temperature, and cut into 1-inch chunks.

Fill a large bowl with ice water and set aside. Bring a large pot of lightly salted water to a boil over high heat. Add the beans and cook until bright green and just tender, 3 to 4 minutes. Plunge the beans immediately into the ice water for 2 minutes. Drain well and pat dry. If the beans are larger than haricots verts, cut them on a diagonal into 2-inch lengths.

Put the olives, mustard, lemon peel, garlic, lemon juice, and anchovy paste into a food processor. Pulse several times until finely chopped but not pureed. With the machine running, add the oil in a slow, steady stream to emulsify. The mixture will be thick and should have some visible bits of olive.

In a large bowl, gently toss the chicken and beans with enough dressing to coat well. Add salt and pepper, and toss again. Serve at room temperature on a bed of fresh greens and topped with the cherry tomatoes.

blanchard's table at blanchard's table at blanchard's table at blanchard's table at blanchard's table at blanchard's table at blanchard's table at blanchard's tab

62

Lemon Shrimp Salad with Asian Greens and Bean Thread Noodles

* SERVES 8

THIS IS A PRETTY DISH WITH LOTS OF TEXTURE. WE LIKE TO ARRANGE IT ON A LARGE YELLOW PLATTER AS AN EXTRAVAGANT SIDE DISH AT BARBECUES.

2 pounds	large shrimp
2 ounces	Chinese bean thread noodles
1/2 cup	olive oil
1/3 cup	freshly squeezed lemon juice
1 teaspoon	salt
1/2 teaspoon	freshly ground black pepper
6 cups	thinly sliced bok choy leaves
1	red bell pepper, seeded and cut into thin strips
4	scallions (white and green parts), thinly sliced
1/4 cup	chopped fresh cilantro, optional
	Salt and freshly ground black pepper

In a large pot, bring 4 quarts of lightly salted water to a boil. Add the unpeeled shrimp, cover, and cook over medium heat until pink and firm, about 2 minutes. Using a slotted spoon, transfer the shrimp to a bowl to cool.

Soak the noodles in a bowl of hot water for 20 minutes. Drain well and pat dry.

Peel the shrimp and slice in half lengthwise. In a small bowl, whisk together the oil, lemon juice, salt, and pepper. Toss the noodles with just enough of the dressing to coat and let sit for 10 minutes. In another bowl, toss the bok choy, red pepper, scallions, shrimp, and cilantro with enough dressing to coat. Season with salt and pepper.

Arrange the noodles on a serving platter or on individual plates and top with the shrimp and vegetables. Serve immediately.

salads and dressings salads and dressings salads and dressings salads and dressings salads and dressings salads and dressings salads and dressings salads and dres

67

Grilled Portobello Mushrooms Stacked with Spinach and Shaved Parmesan

✳ SERVES 4

AT BLANCHARD'S, WE MAKE SO MANY OF THESE MUSHROOMS THAT IT'S HARD TO IMAGINE EVER TAKING THEM OFF THE MENU. THE SUBSTANTIAL FLAVOR OF GRILLED PORTOBELLOS, SHAVINGS OF PARMESAN, AND SPINACH TOSSED WITH A VINAIGRETTE MAKE THIS BOTH COMFORT FOOD AND SUMMER GARDEN FARE ALL AT ONCE.

8	**portobello mushroom caps**
	Olive oil, for grilling
2 handfuls	**spinach, trimmed, rinsed, and dried**
	Lemon-Pepper Vinaigrette (page 80)
2 ounces	**Parmesan cheese, shaved with a vegetable peeler**
12	**cherry tomatoes, cut in half**

HUGHES

Prepare the grill or preheat the broiler.

Brush the mushrooms with oil and grill until tender, 3 to 4 minutes. Toss the spinach with just enough vinaigrette to coat the leaves.

Stack the ingredients on salad plates starting with a small pile of spinach, then a layer of shaved Parmesan, then a mushroom. Repeat the layers in the same order, pressing down gently to keep the stack from falling. Drizzle a little extra vinaigrette over the salads, garnish with the cherry tomato halves, and serve while the mushrooms are still warm.

blanchard's table **at blanchard's table** at blanchard's table **at blanchard's table** at blanchard's table **at blanchard's table** at blanchard's table **at blanchard's tab**

70

Caesar Salad with Homemade Parmesan Croutons

✳ SERVES 6 TO 8

THIS IS CLEARLY NOT A TRADITIONAL CAESAR RECIPE. HOWEVER, IT AVOIDS THE PROBLEMS ASSOCIATED WITH USING RAW EGGS, HAS ALL THE RIGHT FLAVORS, AND IT IS A BREEZE TO MAKE. DON'T BE PUT OFF BY ITS SIMPLICITY—IT TASTES GREAT!

½	**baguette, sliced ¼ inch thick**
¼ **cup**	**olive oil**
⅓ **cup plus** ½ **cup**	**freshly grated Parmesan cheese**
3 heads	**romaine lettuce (or 6 romaine hearts)**
	Caesar Dressing (recipe follows)

Preheat the oven to 400°F.

In a medium bowl, toss the bread with the oil. Arrange on a sheet pan and sprinkle with ⅓ cup Parmesan cheese. Bake until golden brown, 10 to 15 minutes.

Tear the romaine into pieces and toss in a large bowl with enough dressing to coat. Add ½ cup Parmesan cheese and toss again. Just before serving, break the croutons into bite-size pieces and scatter over the salad.

N O T E : Depending on the size of your baguette, you may not want to use all of the croutons in the salad. They will keep at room temperature in an airtight container for 3 days.

WE'VE USED A PEPPER MILL for as long as we can remember, and while working on this book we typed *freshly ground black pepper* more than any other phrase. It made us wonder if there could really be such a big difference between freshly ground and store-bought pepper. So just for fun, we bought a jar of ground black pepper to compare. Freshly ground won hands down— now we know for sure it was worth the typing. Using a pepper grinder with an adjustable top screw allows you to adjust the grind from fine to coarse.

blanchard's table **at blanchard's table** at blanchard's table **at blanchard's table** at blanchard's table **at blanchard's table** at blanchard's table **at blanchard's table** at blanchard's table **at blanchard's tab**

72

Caesar Dressing

✳ MAKES ABOUT 1¼ CUPS

THIS DRESSING WILL KEEP IN THE REFRIGERATOR FOR AT LEAST A WEEK.

1 cup	**Hellmann's mayonnaise**
¾ teaspoon	**anchovy paste**
1 teaspoon	**Worcestershire sauce**
3½ tablespoons	**freshly squeezed lemon juice**
3 medium	**garlic cloves, minced**
¾ teaspoon	**coarsely cracked black pepper**

Put all the ingredients into a medium bowl and whisk until well blended.

N O T E : Look for anchovy paste in convenient tubes. They keep for months in the refrigerator.

salads and dressings salads and dressings salads and dressings salads and dressings salads and dressings salads and dressings salads and dressings salads and dres

73

Roasted Beet Salad with Cranberry Vinaigrette and Blue Cheese

✳ SERVES 6 TO 8

THE FIRST TIME WE ROASTED BEETS, IT WAS LIKE DISCOVERING AN ENTIRELY NEW VEGETABLE. AT BLANCHARD'S, WE NOW ROAST BEETS EVERY DAY. THEIR FLAVOR IS SO MUCH MORE INTENSE THAN WHEN BOILED OR STEAMED, WE'VE BEEN HOOKED EVER SINCE. PLEASE GIVE THEM A TRY. YOU WON'T BE DISAPPOINTED.

8	small beets
1½ tablespoons	apple cider vinegar
3 tablespoons	mild olive oil
½ teaspoon	Dijon mustard
½ cup	whole-berry cranberry sauce (canned is fine)
	Salt and freshly ground black pepper
3 ounces	crumbled blue cheese

Preheat the oven to 400°F.

Cut off the beet greens, leaving on 1 inch of stem, and wrap each beet individually in foil. Roast them on a sheet pan until tender (they'll feel soft when squeezed gently), 1 to 1½ hours. Unwrap and cool to room temperature. Peel and cut into ¼-inch-thick slices.

In a small bowl, whisk together the vinegar, oil, mustard, cranberry sauce, and salt and pepper. Toss the beets with enough dressing to coat and mound on a serving platter or individual plates. Sprinkle with blue cheese and serve at room temperature.

blanchard's table at blanchard's table at blanchard's table at blanchard's table at blanchard's table at blanchard's table at blanchard's table at blanchard's tab

74

Spicy Vegetable Slaw

* SERVES 8 TO 10

HERE'S A COLORFUL, MUSTARDY VERSION OF A SLAW WITH A BIT OF
HEAT FROM THE JALAPEÑOS. THE CARAWAY AND CELERY SEEDS ADD A
SLIGHT CRUNCH TO THE TEXTURE. THIS CAN BE STORED IN THE
REFRIGERATOR FOR SEVERAL DAYS SO IF YOU HAVE EXTRA, KEEP IT
AROUND TO SPICE UP SANDWICHES.

1¼ cups	Hellmann's mayonnaise
3 tablespoons	Dijon mustard
2	fresh jalapeño peppers, seeded and minced
1 tablespoon	sugar
2 tablespoons	white wine vinegar
6 drops	Tabasco sauce
2 teaspoons	freshly grated lemon peel
1 teaspoon	caraway seeds
2 teaspoons	celery seeds
½ teaspoon	salt
½ teaspoon	freshly ground black pepper
1 cup	shredded white cabbage
1 cup	shredded red cabbage
1 cup	shredded or julienned carrots
1	red bell pepper, seeded and julienned
1	yellow bell pepper, seeded and julienned

In a medium bowl, whisk together the mayonnaise, mustard, jalapeño peppers, sugar, vinegar, Tabasco, lemon peel, caraway seeds, celery seeds, salt,
and pepper. Add all the vegetables, toss, and serve chilled.

N O T E : For a less spicy version, omit the jalapeño peppers and cut
back on the black pepper.

Parmesan-Pepper Dressing

✳ MAKES 1½ CUPS

THIS IS BOB'S FAVORITE DRESSING. BEING A SEVENTH-GENERATION
VERMONTER, HE'S QUICK TO REMIND ME THAT HE WAS RAISED ON
MEAT AND POTATOES AND NEVER ATE ANYTHING GREEN UNTIL HE
MET ME. I'M NOT SURE THAT'S ENTIRELY TRUE, BUT HE DOES ADMIT
THAT IF HIS MOTHER HAD KNOWN ABOUT THIS RECIPE SHE MIGHT
HAVE BEEN MORE APT TO BUY A HEAD OF LETTUCE.

¼ cup	freshly squeezed lemon juice
1 cup	freshly grated Parmesan cheese
1	garlic clove
½ cup	milk
1 teaspoon	Worcestershire sauce
1 cup	olive oil
½ teaspoon	salt
½ teaspoon	coarsely cracked black pepper
1 tablespoon	minced fresh oregano or 1 teaspoon dried
2 tablespoons	minced fresh parsley

Put the lemon juice, Parmesan, garlic, milk, and Worcestershire sauce in a food processor, and pulse until the mixture is fairly smooth. With the machine running, add the oil slowly until the dressing is emulsified.

Add the salt, pepper, oregano, and parsley, and pulse twice to blend.

Beyond Maple Syrup

CHANCES ARE THAT WHEN you think of food in Vermont, images of maple syrup, apple cider, and Cheddar cheese come to mind. But did you know that tucked in and around our mountains are approximately six hundred farms producing everything from Camembert and blue cheese to free-range chicken and rainbow trout? Rolling green fields are dotted with apple orchards and there are hundreds of roadside farm stands selling sweet corn, tender Bibb lettuce, and some of the sweetest strawberries you've ever tasted.

Saveur magazine called Vermont the "Coolest Food State in the Union." Visit a restaurant in Vermont and you're likely to get vegetables and berries picked that same morning. A dedicated group of food lovers formed the Vermont Fresh Network, celebrating the relationship between farmers and restaurants throughout the state. They've created a venue in which chefs can be in constant contact with producers of everything from heirloom tomatoes to crusty loaves of bread and award-winning goat cheese.

Our own farmer's market in Norwich is one of New England's best. We try not to miss a Saturday, and the stands are so tempting that we usually end up buying more than we need. In addition to an amazing

. . . pies are sometimes still warm from the oven.

selection of vegetables, fruits, and herbs picked only hours before, you'll find locally produced maple syrup, cheese, and honey, as well as organic beef, chicken, and lamb. Bread, pastries, and cookies are everywhere and pies are sometimes still warm from the oven.

Several stands sell coffee, so we usually pick up a steaming hot cup and a giant soft ginger cookie as we stroll around the market. Since it is very close to the Connecticut River, on spring mornings there's often a cool, wispy layer of fog from the water. Our hands stay happily wrapped around the warm cups as we shop. Later in the season our cups are filled with cider and we treat ourselves to cinnamon pastries filled with local raspberries.

A handsome team of workhorses circles the perimeter of the market pulling wagonloads of children, and the sounds of a hammered dulcimer come from the center gazebo where more children are dancing and spinning on the grass. Craftspeople come from all the surrounding towns to sell their quilts, note cards and furniture. A morning at the farmer's market makes us wish summer in Vermont lasted more than just a few short months.

Homemade Ranch Dressing

DAN & WHIT'S IS THE GENERAL STORE IN OUR HOMETOWN OF
NORWICH, VERMONT. IT'S A TRUE COUNTRY STORE WITH GROCERIES,
HARDWARE, GRAIN, A MEAT COUNTER, AND A SHOE DEPARTMENT.
DAN & WHIT'S HAS LOYALLY CARRIED BLANCHARD & BLANCHARD
SALAD DRESSINGS SINCE WE STARTED MAKING THEM.

IT NEVER OCCURRED TO US THAT PEOPLE ASSUMED WE ALWAYS
MADE ALL OUR OWN DRESSINGS, EVEN AT HOME. THEN WE RAN INTO
OUR DENTIST AT THE DAN & WHIT'S CHECKOUT COUNTER AND FELT
HIM STARING AT OUR BOTTLE OF HIDDEN VALLEY RANCH SALAD
DRESSING. IT WAS THEN WE DECIDED TO MAKE OUR OWN.

1 cup	**buttermilk**
1 cup	**Hellmann's mayonnaise**
1 tablespoon	**Dijon mustard**
2 tablespoons	**freshly squeezed lemon juice**
¼ cup	**finely minced scallions (white and green parts)**
½ teaspoon	**dried tarragon**
½ teaspoon	**dried oregano**
1 teaspoon	**sugar**
¾ teaspoon	**salt**
	Generous grinding of coarse black pepper

In a medium bowl, whisk all the ingredients together.

WE ALWAYS have
three or four mason
jars with salad
dressings in the
refrigerator at any one
time, ready to shake
and pour over greens,
vegetables, or pasta.

Rice Wine Vinaigrette with Ginger

✳ MAKES 1 CUP

HERE'S A REFRESHING ASIAN DRESSING THAT'S BOTH EASY AND
VERSATILE. AT BLANCHARD'S, WE SERVE IT AS A DIPPING SAUCE WITH
LOBSTER DUMPLINGS OR SPRING ROLLS. IN VERMONT, BOB ADDS IT
TO HIS WOK WHEN HE STIR-FRIES SHRIMP AND NOODLES.

¼ cup	rice wine vinegar
¼ cup	red wine vinegar
3 tablespoons	soy sauce
¼ cup	sesame oil
1½ tablespoons	sugar
2 tablespoons	hoisin sauce
1 tablespoon	minced peeled fresh ginger
1 medium	garlic clove, minced

Place all the ingredients into a small mixing bowl and whisk to blend.

Blue Cheese Vinaigrette

✳ MAKES 1¼ CUPS

IF YOU'RE A FAN OF BLUE CHEESE, THIS DRESSING IS FOR YOU. THE
FLAVOR IS HEARTY AND DELICIOUS, AND WE LOVE TO SPOON IT OVER
MASHED POTATOES, SALADS, OR GRILLED HAMBURGERS.

⅓ cup	balsamic vinegar
1	garlic clove, minced
½ teaspoon	salt
½ teaspoon	freshly ground black pepper
⅔ cup	olive oil
3 tablespoons	crumbled blue cheese

In a small bowl, whisk together the vinegar, garlic, salt, and pepper. Gradually whisk in the oil until well blended. Add the blue cheese and whisk
again.

salads and dressings salads and dressings salads and dressings salads and dressings salads and dressings salads and dressings salads and dressings salads and dre

85

Seafood

In a Hurry

Lemon Swordfish with Chives

Sauté swordfish steaks in a pan over medium-high heat with 3 tablespoons olive oil, 3 tablespoons fresh chives, 2 teaspoons freshly grated lemon peel, salt, and a few grindings of black pepper.

Salmon with Ginger and Lemon

Peel 2 lemons, slice thinly, remove their seeds, and set aside. Heat a large sauté pan with 1 tablespoon olive oil, 1 tablespoon butter, and 1 tablespoon minced peeled fresh ginger. Add the lemons and cook for 1 minute. Add 4 salmon fillets and cook to desired doneness, 3 to 4 minutes on each side. Sprinkle with salt and pepper, and serve immediately.

There's Nothing Like a Big Bowl of Mussels

Place 2 cups white wine, 2 tablespoons minced peeled fresh ginger, 2 teaspoons freshly grated lemon peel, and 1 teaspoon dried thyme in a large stockpot. Bring to a boil, add 2½ pounds of cleaned mussels, cover, and cook until all of the shells have opened, 3 to 4 minutes. Discard any shells that have not opened. Toss with 3 tablespoons fresh parsley and serve hot.

Grilled Lemons and Limes for Seafood

Next time you're grilling fish, cut a few lemons or limes in half and grill them cut side down, until brown, 1 to 2 minutes. Squeeze the warm juice over the fish for a delightful change. The acidity found in the raw fruit turns into an almost sweet-sour flavor when grilled.

Shrimp with Green Peppercorns and Mustard

Marinate 2 pounds of peeled and deveined large shrimp in a mixture of 2 tablespoons white wine vinegar, ½ cup orange juice, ⅓ cup olive oil, 1 teaspoon Dijon mustard, 3 tablespoons drained green peppercorns, 2 tablespoons chopped parsley, ½ teaspoon salt, and ¼ teaspoon black pepper. Grill or broil until done, about 2 minutes on each side.

CLINTON

88

Quick Seafood Stew with Tomatoes and Herbs

* SERVES 4

DON'T LET THE LONG LIST OF INGREDIENTS PREVENT YOU FROM MAK-
ING THIS RECIPE. IT'S REALLY QUITE SIMPLE, AND WITH A LOAF
OF CRUSTY BREAD AND A SALAD IT MAKES A BEAUTIFUL DINNER FOR
FAMILY OR COMPANY.

¼ cup	olive oil
4	scallions (white and green parts), thinly sliced
1	large yellow onion, cut in half and thinly sliced
1	red bell pepper, seeded and coarsely chopped
2	garlic cloves, thinly sliced
2 14½-ounce cans	Italian stewed tomatoes
2 cups	bottled clam juice
1 teaspoon	dried oregano
1 teaspoon	dried basil
12	shrimp, peeled, deveined, and tails left on
12	sea scallops
12	littleneck clams, scrubbed
¾ pound	firm white fish, cut into 1-inch pieces (swordfish works well)
	Salt and freshly ground black pepper
3 tablespoons	chopped fresh parsley

Heat the oil in a large pot over medium-high heat, and add the scallions, onion, pepper, and garlic. Cook, stirring occasionally, until the onion is golden, about 10 minutes. Add the tomatoes and break them up slightly with a spoon. Add the clam juice, oregano, and basil; then cover and bring to a boil. Uncover and simmer for 10 minutes, or until slightly thickened.

Add the shrimp, scallops, clams, and fish. Cover and simmer until the fish and shellfish are cooked through and the clams have opened, 5 to 10 minutes. Taste for salt and pepper and ladle into shallow bowls. Sprinkle with parsley and serve immediately.

food seaf

91

Sweet-and-Sour Swordfish with Onions, Raisins, and Tomatoes

✳ SERVES 4

THE SWORDFISH HERE CAN BE GRILLED, PAN SEARED, OR BROILED.
IT'S THE SAUCE THAT MAKES THE DISH, SO COOK THE SWORDFISH
ANY WAY YOU LIKE. THE LIME JUICE CREATES A SUBTLE CONTRAST
WITH THE BROWN SUGAR AND RAISINS, AND THE BRILLIANT COLOR
OF THE TOMATO-BASED SAUCE LENDS ITSELF TO A SIMPLE SIDE OF
ROASTED POTATOES OR COUSCOUS.

¼ cup	olive oil
2	large yellow onions, thinly sliced
⅓ cup	dry white wine
2 teaspoons	dried oregano
2 cups	canned whole plum tomatoes with their juice
¼ cup	raisins
2 tablespoons	brown sugar
2 tablespoons	freshly squeezed lime juice
½ teaspoon	salt
¼ teaspoon	freshly ground black pepper
¼ cup	chopped fresh parsley
4	swordfish steaks (each about 8 ounces and 1 inch thick)

In a large pot, heat 2 tablespoons of the oil over medium-low heat and
cook the onions until soft but not brown. Add the wine, reduce the heat,
and cook until all the liquid is absorbed and the onions are very soft.
Increase the heat to medium, add the oregano, and cook for 2 minutes.

Add the tomatoes with their juice and break them into pieces using a
long spoon. Bring to a boil, then simmer gently until thickened, 4 to 5 minutes. Add the raisins, brown sugar, lime juice, salt, pepper, and parsley.

Brush the swordfish with the remaining olive oil, sprinkle it with salt
and pepper, and cook on the grill, in a sauté pan, or under the broiler for
about 5 minutes on each side. Divide the sauce onto four dinner plates and
place a piece of swordfish on each.

blanchard's table at blanchard's table at blanchard's table at blanchard's table at blanchard's table at blanchard's table at blanchard's table at blanchard's tab

94

Grilled Mahimahi with Mild Red Thai Curry Sauce

* SERVES 4

AT BLANCHARD'S WE SERVE THIS FISH ON A BED OF SAUTÉED CORN, SHIITAKE MUSHROOMS, AND SPINACH. AT HOME, THE SAUCE BECOMES AN ALL-PURPOSE ADDITION FOR GRILLED CHICKEN AND SHRIMP.

3 tablespoons	peanut oil
1	garlic clove, minced
1½ teaspoons	minced peeled fresh ginger
2 teaspoons	curry powder
2 teaspoons	Thai red curry paste
2 teaspoons	paprika
¾ teaspoon	ground cumin
2 tablespoons	soy sauce
2 tablespoons	tomato puree
2 tablespoons	packed light brown sugar
1 14-ounce can	unsweetened coconut milk
4	mahimahi fillets (8 ounces each)
	Olive oil, for grilling
	Salt and freshly ground black pepper

Prepare the grill.

Measure all the ingredients and have them ready by the stove. In a large saucepan, heat the oil over medium heat. Add the garlic and ginger, and cook for 1 minute. Reduce the heat to low, and add the curry powder, curry paste, paprika, and cumin. Stir and cook for 2 minutes.

Raise the heat back to medium, and add the soy sauce, tomato puree, brown sugar, and coconut milk, whisking well after each addition. When small bubbles form around the edge of the saucepan, simmer very gently for 10 minutes, whisking frequently. Do not allow it to boil.

Brush the mahimahi with olive oil, sprinkle with salt and pepper, and grill until cooked through. Serve immediately with the sauce.

WHEN A RECIPE calls for grilling, you can always use a broiler or a grill pan on your stove instead. If you don't have a grill pan, we'd recommend giving one a try. Ours is a coated cast-iron version made by Le Creuset. It spans two burners, and when preheated for 5 minutes, sears meat and fish beautifully.

food seafood seafood seafood seafood seafood seafood seafood seafood seafood seafood seafood seafood seafood seafood seafood seafood seafood seaf

99

Meat

* In a Hurry

   Balsamic Pepper Puree ▪ Dijon and Shallot Cream ▪ Horseradish Sauce ▪
   Ruby Red Currant Sauce ▪ Sun-Dried Tomato Puree ▪ Orient Express
   ▪ Mustard Sauce with Capers and Parmesan ▪ Balsamic Sauce with
   Scallions ▪ Coconut-Lime Sauce

* Vermont Chicken and Biscuits

* Quick Chicken Breasts with Bacon, Marsala, Peas, and Cream

* Lemon-Pepper Chicken

* Pan-Roasted Chicken with Lemon, Olives, and Rosemary

* Barbecued Chicken

* Calypso Chicken with Lime

* Coconut Curried Chicken

* Shepherd's Pie

* Beef Tenderloin with Green Curry, Red Pepper, Peas, and Scallions

* Beef and Guinness Stew with Carrots and Sautéed Mushrooms

* Veal Chops Crusted with Mustard, Mango, and Oregano

* Grilled Veal Chops with Rosemary and Lemon

* Balsamic-Glazed Veal Chops

* Double-Rib Lamb Chops with Hoisin Sesame Sauce

* Vermont Picnic Ham Baked in Dark Beer

Pan-Roasted Chicken with Lemon, Olives, and Rosemary

✳ SERVES 4

VERMONT AND TUSCANY HAVE A LOT IN COMMON: ROLLING HILLS, ANCIENT FARMS, GREEN FIELDS, AND SMALL TOWNS. OF COURSE, IN TUSCANY THE MAPLE TREES WOULD BE OLIVE TREES AND THE CORNFIELDS WOULD BE VINEYARDS. NONETHELESS, THE THOUGHTS INSPIRED US TO MAKE THIS DISH, WHICH REMINDED US OF OUR LAST VISIT TO SIENA.

THE DEEPLY FLAVORED SAUCE WITH THIS CHICKEN IS LOADED WITH CHARACTER. IT SEEPS INTO THE MEAT AS IT SIMMERS AND RESULTS IN AN ALMOST STEWLIKE DISH. ADD EVEN MORE OLIVES IF YOU LIKE SOME IN EVERY BITE.

1	3-pound chicken, cut into 8 pieces
½ cup	all-purpose flour
2 tablespoons	olive oil
2	garlic cloves, thinly sliced
2	shallots, thinly sliced
3 cups	chicken broth
1 cup	dry white wine
1 tablespoon	freshly grated lemon peel
3 tablespoons	fresh rosemary leaves
1 cup	pitted green olives, cut in half
	Salt and freshly ground black pepper

Dredge the chicken in the flour and set aside. In a large sauté pan, heat the oil over high heat and cook the chicken until crisp and brown, 2 to 3 minutes on each side.

Add the garlic, shallots, broth, wine, lemon peel, and rosemary, and bring to a boil. Reduce the heat, cover, and simmer for 30 minutes. Add the olives and simmer uncovered for 20 to 30 minutes, or until the chicken is cooked through and the sauce has developed some body.

Taste for salt and pepper, and serve immediately.

at blanchard's table at blanchard's table at blanchard's table at blanchard's table at blanchard's table at blanchard's table at blanchard's table at blanchard's tab

114

Coconut Curried Chicken

LADLE THIS OVER A GENEROUS SERVING OF STEAMED JASMINE RICE.
WITH A LOAF OF GOOD BREAD IT MAKES A GREAT ONE-BOWL MEAL.
ADD MORE RED CURRY PASTE FOR EXTRA SPICE.

1 tablespoon	Thai red curry paste
2 cups	sweet potato, peeled and cut into 1-inch chunks
2 pounds	boneless, skinless chicken breast halves, cut into 1-inch chunks
2 cups	chicken broth
1½ cups	unsweetened coconut milk
2	scallions (white and green parts), cut into 1-inch pieces
2 heads	baby bok choy (white and green parts), cut into 1-inch pieces
½ cup	shiitake mushroom caps
1 tablespoon	olive oil
	Salt
	Fresh cilantro leaves, for garnish

Heat a large pot over medium-high heat. Add the curry paste and cook 1 to 2 minutes, or until fragrant. Add the sweet potato and chicken and cook for 2 minutes. Stir in the broth and coconut milk, reduce the heat to low, and simmer gently until the chicken and sweet potato are cooked, 15 to 20 minutes.

Meanwhile, prepare the vegetables. Bring a pot of lightly salted water to a boil. Blanch the scallions and bok choy in the boiling water until bright green and crisp-tender, 1 to 2 minutes, then drain. If the shiitakes are bite size, keep them whole. If not, cut them into halves or quarters. Heat the oil in a small sauté pan and cook the mushrooms quickly, just to soften.

Just before serving, add the scallions, bok choy, and mushrooms to the chicken pot. Season with salt and serve immediately garnished with cilantro.

at meat meat meat meat meat meat meat meat meat meat meat meat meat meat meat meat meat meat meat meat meat meat meat meat meat meat meat meat meat meat meat

Balsamic-Glazed Veal Chops

* SERVES 4

THIS DISH IS SO EASY IT FEELS FUNNY WRITING DOWN THE RECIPE.
BUT EVERY TIME WE SERVE THESE CHOPS TO COMPANY WE GET GREAT
REVIEWS, SO HERE IT IS.

1/2 cup	olive oil
2/3 cup	balsamic vinegar
4	veal chops (each about 12 ounces)
	Salt and freshly ground black pepper

Prepare the grill or preheat the broiler.

Combine the oil and vinegar in a small bowl, and pour half of it into a shallow dish. Place the veal chops in the dish, coat well with the marinade, and let sit for 30 minutes.

Grill the veal chops to desired doneness, basting with the reserved half of the oil and vinegar mixture. Cook for about 3 minutes on each side for medium. Sprinkle with salt and pepper, and serve immediately.

meat meat meat meat meat meat meat meat meat meat meat meat meat meat meat meat meat meat meat meat meat meat meat meat meat

Pasta

* Linguine with Swordfish, Roasted Cherry Tomatoes, and Balsamic Vinegar
* In a Hurry
* Spaghetti with Chicken, Lemon, and Mushrooms
* B.L.T. Fusilli
* Four-Cheese Fettuccine with Chives
* Fusilli with Spinach, Tomatoes, and Mozzarella
* Penne with Sun-Dried Tomatoes, Capers, and Olives
* Bow Ties with Bacon, Peas, and Parmesan
* Penne with Shrimp, Garlic, Lemon, and Basil

Spaghetti with Chicken, Lemon, and Mushrooms

* SERVES 4 TO 6

THIS RECIPE CALLS FOR COOKED CHICKEN. WE USUALLY SIMMER SEVERAL BREASTS IN CHICKEN BROTH FOR ABOUT 15 MINUTES, BUT LEFTOVER ROAST CHICKEN WILL DO JUST FINE.

1 pound	spaghetti
3 tablespoons	olive oil
2	garlic cloves, minced
1 pound	white mushrooms, thinly sliced
1½ pounds	boneless chicken breast halves, cooked and thinly sliced
1 tablespoon	freshly grated lemon peel
¼ cup	freshly squeezed lemon juice
½ cup	chopped fresh basil or 2 tablespoons dried
2 teaspoons	dried red pepper flakes
	Salt and freshly ground black pepper
	Plenty of freshly grated Parmesan cheese

Bring a large pot of lightly salted water to a boil over high heat. Add the spaghetti and cook until tender. Drain well and return to the pot.

While the spaghetti is cooking, heat the oil in a large sauté pan over high heat. Add the garlic and mushrooms, and cook until the mushrooms are lightly browned, 2 to 3 minutes. Add the chicken and cook until heated through.

Add the mushrooms and chicken, lemon peel, lemon juice, basil, and pepper flakes to the spaghetti, and toss well. Taste for salt and pepper. Serve immediately with Parmesan cheese.

ANY OF OUR pasta recipes would make an excellent first course if served in smaller portions.

sta past

135

Fusilli with Spinach, Tomatoes, and Mozzarella

* SERVES 4

ADDING SPINACH TO PASTA IS A GREAT IDEA. IT GIVES A SIMPLE DISH
SOME COMPLEXITY AND COLOR WITH LITTLE EFFORT.

1 pound	fusilli
3 tablespoons	olive oil
2	large yellow onions, chopped
1 14-ounce can	whole Italian plum tomatoes with their juice
2/3 cup	pitted kalamata olives, sliced
1 pound	spinach leaves, stems removed
3/4 cup	chopped fresh basil
1/2 pound	fresh mozzarella, thinly sliced
1 1/2 teaspoons	salt
1/2 teaspoon	freshly ground black pepper
	Freshly grated Parmesan cheese

Bring a large pot of lightly salted water to a boil over high heat. Add the fusilli and cook until tender. Drain well and return to the pot.

While the fusilli is cooking, heat the oil in a large sauté pan over medium-high heat. Add the onion and cook until soft and lightly browned, 5 to 6 minutes. Add the tomatoes and cut them into smaller pieces with a spoon. Simmer until heated through.

Once the fusilli is back in the pasta pot, turn the heat to medium and add the tomatoes, olives, spinach, and basil, and toss well. As soon as the spinach leaves are slightly wilted, 2 to 3 minutes, toss the mozzarella with the pasta and remove from the heat. Taste for salt and pepper, and serve immediately with Parmesan cheese.

pasta pas

139

Vegetables and Sides

* Island Rice with Cumin and Coconut
* In a Hurry
    Roasted Sweet Potato Wedges ▪ Lemon-Asiago Asparagus ▪
    Broiled Mangoes ▪ Roasted Curried Sweet Potatoes ▪ Cheesy
    Prosciutto-Wrapped Asparagus ▪ Roasted Onion ▪ Maple Mashed
    Sweet Potatoes
* Roasted Potatoes with Chives and Parmesan
* Lowell's Curried Rice with Vegetables
* Caribbean Corn Bread
* Yellow Squash with Shallots, Sun-Dried Tomatoes, and Basil
* Baked Onions with Rye Bread and Cheddar
* Mashed Baked Potatoes
* Melted Balsamic Onions
* Parsnips with Rosemary and Parmesan
* Balsamic Asparagus
* Sweet-and-Sour Red Cabbage
* Marinated Red and Yellow Peppers
* Jasmine Rice Cakes with Toasted Sesame Seeds
* Sweet Potato Puree
* Tomato Couscous
* Cranberry-Jalapeño Relish
* Wild Mushroom and Corn Medley

Roasted Potatoes with Chives and Parmesan

✳ SERVES 4 TO 6

SERVE THESE MELT-IN-YOUR-MOUTH POTATOES RIGHT FROM THE OVEN.

2 pounds	red-skinned potatoes, cut into large chunks
2 tablespoons	olive oil
1 teaspoon	salt
¼ teaspoon	freshly ground black pepper
2 tablespoons	chopped fresh chives
3 tablespoons	freshly grated Parmesan cheese

Preheat the oven to 400°F.

Toss the potatoes with the oil, salt, and pepper on a sheet pan or in a large gratin dish. Roast until browned and tender, tossing the potatoes occasionally with a spatula, about 45 minutes to 1 hour.

Transfer the hot potatoes to a serving bowl, and toss with the chives and Parmesan cheese. Serve immediately.

t blanchard's table **at blanchard's table** at blanchard's table at blanchard's table **at blanchard's table** at blanchard's table **at blanchard's table** at blanchard's table **at blanchard's tab**

150

Caribbean Corn Bread

* SERVES 8

HERE'S A RECIPE THAT WILL CHANGE YOUR OPINION ABOUT CORN-BREAD FOREVER. MOIST AND RICH, THIS HAS KERNELS OF CORN, MONTEREY JACK CHEESE, AND BITS OF JUICY PINEAPPLE. WE MAKE IT AT HOME BARBECUES AND ALWAYS SERVE IT ON THANKSGIVING IN THE RESTAURANT.

1 cup	all-purpose flour
1 cup	cornmeal
2 tablespoons	baking powder
1 teaspoon	salt
½ pound (2 sticks)	unsalted butter, at room temperature
¾ cup	sugar
4	eggs
1½ cups	canned cream-style corn
½ cup	canned crushed pineapple, drained
1 cup	shredded Monterey Jack or mild white Cheddar cheese

Preheat the oven to 325°F.

Butter and flour a 9-inch square glass cake pan. (You can use a metal cake pan, but we've found the old-fashioned glass Pyrex brand works best.)

In a medium bowl, whisk together the flour, corn meal, baking powder, and salt, and set aside.

In a mixer, cream the butter and sugar. While the mixer is running, add the eggs one at a time, beating well after each addition. Add the corn, pineapple, and cheese, and mix to blend. On a low speed, add the dry ingredients and mix until blended well.

Pour the batter into the prepared pan and bake until golden brown around the edges and a tester stuck in the center comes out clean, about 1 hour.

ONE OF OUR LOYAL CUSTOMERS is a man named Mr. Wilson. He comes to Anguilla every year in late November and traditionally eats Thanksgiving dinner at Blanchard's. Mr. Wilson *loves* our corn bread and we usually pack up a small pan of it for him to take along for breakfast the next day. One year, Mr. Wilson came later than usual and missed the corn bread. We would have made him a special batch, but there was no more creamed corn to be found in Anguilla. Now, every November, four cans of creamed corn appear on our doorstep—our signal that Mr. Wilson has arrived on the island.

getables and sides **vegetables and sides** vegetables and sides **vegetables and sides** vegetables and sides **vegetables and sides** vegetables and sides **vegetables and**

155

Jasmine Rice Cakes with Toasted Sesame Seeds

✳ SERVES 6 TO 8

WE LOVE THIS RECIPE. THE CAKES GET BROWN AND CRISPY ON THE OUTSIDE AND HAVE ALMOST A CREAMY TEXTURE WITH A HINT OF COCONUT INSIDE. THEY ARE GREAT FOR SOAKING UP THE FLAVOR OF A BOLD SAUCE, PARTICULARLY ONE WITH SOY SAUCE OR OTHER ASIAN INGREDIENTS.

3¾ cups	water
¾ cup	unsweetened coconut milk, well mixed
2¼ cups	jasmine rice
¾ teaspoon	salt
	Generous grinding of black pepper
3	scallions (white and green parts), chopped
2 tablespoons	toasted sesame seeds
	Olive oil
	Dry, unflavored bread crumbs

Bring the water and coconut milk to a boil in a large pot. Add the rice, salt, and pepper as soon as the water boils. Cover and reduce the heat to very low. Cook until the water is absorbed, about 20 minutes.

When the rice is cooked, transfer to a large bowl. Mix in the scallions and toasted sesame seeds. Press the mixture into a 9 × 12-inch sheet pan. Cover with plastic wrap and roll a bottle over the top to make it firm and compact. Press down evenly, making the surface flat and smooth. Chill thoroughly.

To serve, cut the chilled rice into 3-inch squares and then cut the squares diagonally in half to form triangles. Brush lightly with oil, coat with bread crumbs, and sauté over medium heat on both sides until golden.

etables and sides vegetables and sides vegetables and sides vegetables and sides vegetables and sides vegetables and sides vegetables and sides vegetables and

167

The Family That Cooks Together . . .

IF WE COULD CLOSE OUR EYES and make a wish for America, we'd create a time every single week for families to gather together. We don't mean shop at the mall or watch a movie. The one and only purpose for such a gathering would be to enjoy each other's company. Plain and simple.

Picture this: your entire family—be it two, three, or more people—eagerly spending every Sunday afternoon together. *Eagerly* is the key word here. You'd laugh and share stories about girlfriends and boyfriends, neighbors, people at work, thoughts about school, and whatever other topics happened to be on your mind.

Think about how many hours you spend with friends and coworkers compared with those you spend with your family. How many times during the course of a year has your family spent time together just for the sake of being together? Of course you gather for holidays and celebrations. That's a given. But we're talking about time when there's nothing to celebrate except the fact that you are a family.

One of the questions we're most frequently asked is how we became so interested in food. Our answer usually surprises people when we say it's all about family.

From the time our son Jesse was small, cooking was the Blanchard family pastime. He could handle chopsticks at age three and we were forming tortellini together when he was six. We tapped maple trees and made maple syrup on the kitchen stove, just as Bob had done with his family when he was young. In the fall, when the leaves in Vermont turn those amazing shades of red, yellow, and orange, we'd go apple picking and return home to make pies, applesauce, and crisps for weeks to come.

As Jesse grew older, it became clear that kitchen time was magical time. We'd pore through cookbooks to find things we all liked and then we'd create them together. The magical part was the

experience of cooking and how it bonded us as a family. It gave us uninterrupted time to share stories and solve problems.

Jesse was rewarded with a sense of accomplishment every time he learned a new skill, and he loved the excitement of tasting new flavors. The food was not always fancy or complicated. Melting cheese for fondue and forming hamburgers for a barbecue were just as much fun as weaving a lattice crust over a blueberry pie. We learned that an amazing family spirit develops in the kitchen.

These lessons taught us not only about building a family but also about building a business. It's no coincidence that out of our eight businesses, the most successful have had kitchens. Those kitchens built strong teams of people who loved their jobs and felt a shared sense of accomplishment as their tasks changed and grew. They talked about the work at hand and the world outside. In every meaningful sense of the word, they formed a family. Today, with the beach right outside our door and palm trees rustling on the roof, the magic of family is again created at our restaurant while we make ice cream, peel onions, simmer soups, and serve food to guests who come to enjoy the experience.

. . . it became clear that kitchen time was magical time.

So when people ask how we became so interested in food and how on earth we had the nerve to open a restaurant, the answer is clear. We wanted our gatherings in the kitchen and at the dining table to become a nightly event, and now they have.

Desserts

* In a Hurry

  It's Berry, Berry Easy ▪ Banana Brûlée ▪ Mama Loves Shortbread and Ice Cream, Too ▪ Frozen Grapes ▪ 10-Minute Caramel Sauce ▪ Kahlúa Espresso Ice Cream ▪ Warm Cranberry-Pear Sundaes

* Lemon Pound Cake Two Ways

* Clinton's Peach Coffee Cake * Cinnamon Maple Wonton Crisps

* Mangoes and Cream

* Rhubarb Coffee Cake * Baked Apples with Cider and Rum

* Light-as-a-Cloud Lemon Mousse

* Glazed Lemon-Pecan Cookies * Chocolate Cookies with Toasted Coconut

* Chewy Oatmeal-Raisin Cookies * Brown Sugar Chocolate Chip Cookies

* World's Best Ginger Cookies

* White Chocolate and Apricot Bread Pudding with Apricot Sauce

* Saucepan Brownies * Coconut Cheesecake

* Warm Summer Fruit Compote with Vanilla Ice Cream

* Extra Thick Hot Fudge Sauce * Chocolate Sauce

* Homemade Coconut Ice Cream * Cracked Coconut

* Sautéed Apricots and Cranberries with Lime, Rum, and Cream

* Vanilla-Poached Peaches with Shredded Coconut and Lemon

* Warm Green Apples with Cinnamon and Ice Cream

* Mocha Fondue

* Very Intense Chocolate Slab with Kahlúa Custard Sauce

* Gingerbread with Warm Cinnamon Bananas and Rum

Lemon Pound Cake Two Ways

* MAKES 2 LOAVES

AT BLANCHARD'S, SOME NIGHTS WE SERVE THIS WARM WITH VANILLA
BEAN ICE CREAM, FRESH BERRIES, AND RASPBERRY SAUCE. ON OTHER
NIGHTS WE SERVE IT WITH COCONUT ICE CREAM AND HOT FUDGE
SAUCE. WHEN WE MAKE IT AT HOME, WE TOAST THE LEFTOVERS IN
THE MORNING TO HAVE WITH COFFEE OR TEA. IT MAKES TWO LOAVES
BUT FREEZES WELL SO YOU CAN KEEP ONE ON HAND FOR A QUICK
DESSERT.

3 cups	all-purpose flour
3/4 teaspoon	salt
1/2 teaspoon	baking powder
1/2 teaspoon	baking soda
1 teaspoon	ground cinnamon
1/2 pound (2 sticks)	unsalted butter, at room temperature and cut into pieces
2 cups	sugar
3 tablespoons	freshly grated lemon peel
4	large eggs, at room temperature
3 tablespoons	freshly squeezed lemon juice
1 tablespoon	vanilla extract
1 cup	buttermilk

Preheat the oven to 350°F.

Butter and flour two 8½ × 4½-inch loaf pans.

In a small bowl, whisk together the flour, salt, baking powder, baking
soda, and cinnamon, and set aside.

With an electric mixer, cream the butter, sugar, and lemon peel until
light and fluffy. Add the eggs, one at a time. Scrape the sides of the bowl to
blend well.

Add the lemon juice and vanilla. Beat until blended—just a few
seconds.

On the lowest speed, alternately add the flour mixture and buttermilk.
Start with about a third of the flour, then add half of the buttermilk, then a
third more flour, then the rest of the buttermilk, then the remaining flour.
Stop mixing just before it is all blended and finish mixing gently by hand
with a rubber spatula. Do not overmix.

Divide the batter into the prepared pans. Bake until golden brown and
a tester inserted into the center comes out clean, 45 to 50 minutes. Serve
warm with ice cream and chocolate sauce or berries.

erts desserts desserts desserts desserts desserts desserts desserts desserts desserts desserts desserts desserts desserts desserts desserts desser

179

Mangoes and Cream

✳ SERVES 4

THIS IS ONE OF OUR EASIEST AND MOST POPULAR DESSERTS.
PEACHES CAN EASILY BE SUBSTITUTED FOR THE MANGOES IF YOU
PREFER.

3 large	ripe mangoes, peeled
1 cup	heavy whipping cream
2 to 3 tablespoons	granulated sugar
1 teaspoon	vanilla extract
	light brown sugar, for sprinkling
	ground cinnamon, for sprinkling

Slice the mangoes into ½-inch thick slices and cut into 1-inch pieces.

Whip the cream with the desired amount of granulated sugar and the vanilla until soft peaks form. Gently fold the mangoes into the cream.

Spoon the mixture into dessert bowls and sprinkle with brown sugar and cinnamon. Serve immediately.

BOB

Light-as-a-Cloud Lemon Mousse

THIS RECIPE DOESN'T TAKE MUCH TIME, BUT FOR AN EASY SHORTCUT, SKIP THE FIRST STEP AND START WITH A GOOD-QUALITY, PURCHASED LEMON CURD. IT WON'T HAVE QUITE THE SAME FRESH, LEMONY ZIP BUT IT'S A SUITABLE ALTERNATIVE.

1 cup	sugar
¾ cup	freshly squeezed lemon juice
6	large egg yolks
2	large eggs
1 tablespoon	freshly grated lemon peel
1½ cups	heavy cream
	Assorted berries and whipped cream, for serving

In the top of a double boiler over simmering water, combine the sugar, lemon juice, egg yolks, eggs, and lemon peel. Cook, whisking constantly, until a thermometer reads 160°F. Transfer to a bowl, cover with plastic wrap, and chill.

When the lemon mixture is cold, whip the cream until soft to medium peaks form. Gently fold a quarter of the whipped cream into the lemon mixture to blend, and then fold in the remaining cream.

Chill in a large serving bowl, or spoon into individual glasses or bowls. Garnish with berries and sweetened whipped cream.

sserts desserts desserts desserts desserts desserts desserts desserts desserts desserts desserts desserts desserts desserts desserts desserts desserts desserts dess

187

Chewy Oatmeal-Raisin Cookies

✳ MAKES 5 DOZEN COOKIES

CLASSIC, SIMPLE, AND DELICIOUS.

2¼ cups	all-purpose flour
1 teaspoon	ground cinnamon
½ teaspoon	salt
1½ teaspoons	baking soda
¾ cup (1½ sticks)	unsalted butter, at room temperature
1½ cups	sugar
2 tablespoons	milk
1	large egg
⅓ cup	molasses
2 cups	old-fashioned rolled oats
1 cup	raisins

Preheat the oven to 350°F.

Line sheet pans with parchment paper.

In a medium bowl, whisk together the flour, cinnamon, salt, and baking soda, and set aside. Using a mixer, cream the butter and sugar until light and fluffy. Add the milk and egg, and beat until blended. Add the molasses and mix to blend. With the mixer on low, add the flour mixture and beat until just barely blended. Stir in the rolled oats and raisins, mixing only until evenly distributed.

Drop the dough by heaping tablespoons about 2 inches apart onto the sheet pans. Bake until the edges are light brown, 10 to 12 minutes.

NOTHING IS QUITE as comforting as a cookie jar filled with homemade cookies. Ours is made of thick apothecary glass so people can see exactly what's inside.

desserts desserts desserts desserts desserts desserts desserts desserts desserts desserts desserts desserts desserts desserts desserts desserts desserts desse

191

Brown Sugar Chocolate Chip Cookies

✳ MAKES 5 DOZEN COOKIES

EVERYBODY LOVES CHOCOLATE CHIP COOKIES AND WE ALL MAKE
THEM DIFFERENTLY. OURS DOESN'T STRAY FAR FROM THE
TRADITIONAL EXCEPT THAT WE USE ONLY BROWN SUGAR. ADD 1 CUP
OF CHOPPED NUTS IF YOU LIKE, BUT DON'T REFRIGERATE THE DOUGH
BEFORE BAKING OR THE TEXTURE WILL BE TOO CAKELIKE.

2½ cups	all-purpose flour
1 teaspoon	baking soda
1 teaspoon	salt
1 cup (2 sticks)	unsalted butter, at room temperature
2 cups	light brown sugar, packed
2	large eggs, at room temperature
1 tablespoon	vanilla extract
2 cups	semisweet chocolate chips

Preheat the oven to 350°F.

Line sheet pans with parchment paper.

In a small bowl, whisk together the flour, baking soda, and salt, and set
aside. Using a mixer, cream the butter and brown sugar until light and
fluffy. Add the eggs, one at a time, beating well after each addition. Add
the vanilla and mix to blend. On low speed, add the flour mixture and mix
until just blended—do not overbeat. Stir in the chocolate chips.

Spoon heaping tablespoons of dough 2 inches apart onto the sheet
pans. Bake until the edges are golden brown, 12 to 15 minutes.

Is IT A COOKIE OR CANDY BAR? We're not great fans of chocolate chip
cookies that are more chocolate than cookie. The balance is important. We
prefer regular-size semisweet morsels to the more trendy chocolate chunks.
The smaller chips allow you to taste more of the cookie itself, which can
easily get overpowered by the larger pieces.

---

t blanchard's table at blanchard's table at blanchard's table at blanchard's table at blanchard's table at blanchard's table at blanchard's table at blanchard's tab

192

World's Best Ginger Cookies

* MAKES 4 DOZEN COOKIES

GINGER COOKIES HAVE BEEN STANDARD FARE IN NEW ENGLAND
KITCHENS FOR DECADES. THIS RECIPE WAS ADAPTED FROM ONE USED
AT STURBRIDGE VILLAGE, WHERE THE COOKIES ARE BAKED IN A
WOOD-FIRED OVEN. THEY'RE ADDICTIVE! IF YOU HAVE ANY LEFT,
CRUMBLE A FEW OVER ICE CREAM FOR AN EASY DESSERT.

2¼ cups	flour
2 teaspoons	ground cinnamon
2 teaspoons	ground ginger
½ teaspoon	ground cloves
2 teaspoons	baking soda
½ teaspoon	salt
1 cup	light brown sugar, packed
1 cup (2 sticks)	unsalted butter, at room temperature
1	large egg, at room temperature
⅓ cup	molasses
½ cup	granulated sugar

Preheat the oven to 325°F.

Line cookie sheets with parchment paper.

In a small bowl, whisk together the flour, cinnamon, ginger, cloves, baking soda, and salt, and set aside.

Using a mixer, cream the brown sugar and butter until light and fluffy. Add the egg and beat until blended. Scrape down the sides of the bowl and add the molasses. With the mixer on low, add the dry ingredients and mix until just blended.

Put ½ cup granulated sugar on a small plate. Roll the dough into 1-inch balls and coat them with sugar. Place the cookie dough 2 inches apart on sheet pans and flatten them slightly with the palm of your hand. Bake 12 to 14 minutes, or until golden brown.

serts desserts desserts desserts desserts desserts desserts desserts desserts desserts desserts desserts desserts desserts desserts desse

193

White Chocolate and Apricot Bread Pudding with Apricot Sauce

✳ SERVES 6 TO 8

WE'VE NEVER BEEN PARTICULARLY FOND OF WHITE CHOCOLATE, BUT IT'S GREAT IN THIS BREAD PUDDING. THE APRICOT SAUCE OFFERS A WELCOME CONTRAST IN FLAVOR AND TAKES ONLY 5 MINUTES TO MAKE.

½ cup	**dried apricots, cut into ¼-inch pieces**
4 medium	**croissants, cut into 1-inch cubes**
2	**large eggs**
7	**large egg yolks**
1 cup	**milk**
3 cups	**heavy cream**
½ cup	**sugar**
10 ounces	**white chocolate, chopped**
1 tablespoon	**vanilla extract**
	Apricot Sauce (recipe follows)
	Whipped cream, for serving

Preheat the oven to 350°F.

Toss the apricots with the croissants and place them in an 8-inch square glass baking dish. In a small bowl, whisk together the eggs and egg yolks and set aside.

In a large pot, combine the milk, cream, and sugar, and scald the mixture over medium-high heat until bubbles form around the edge, 5 to 6 minutes. Stir in the white chocolate and vanilla, and mix until melted. Gradually whisk in the egg mixture. Pour the custard over the croissants and apricots, pressing down gently to cover completely. Let the mixture rest for 15 minutes.

Cover with aluminum foil and place the baking dish in a larger roasting pan. Add enough hot water to come 1 inch up the sides of the baking dish. Bake until firm to the touch, about 1 hour and 15 minutes.

Serve warm with Apricot Sauce and freshly whipped cream.

t blanchard's table at blanchard's table at blanchard's table at blanchard's table at blanchard's table at blanchard's table at blanchard's table at blanchard's tab

194

Apricot Sauce

| 1½ cups | good-quality apricot preserves |
| ⅓ cup | orange juice |

In a food processor, puree the preserves and orange juice. Transfer to a small saucepan over medium heat and simmer gently until the preserves are melted. If the sauce is too thick, add a little more juice.

Warm Summer Fruit Compote with Vanilla Ice Cream

✳ SERVES 6 TO 8

SERVED WARM OR AT ROOM TEMPERATURE, THIS COMPOTE IS SO GREAT YOU CAN EVEN USE FRUITS THAT MAY BE A LITTLE BRUISED OR PAST THEIR PRIME. STORE ANY LEFTOVER COMPOTE IN THE REFRIGERATOR AND ENJOY IT IN THE MORNING FOR BREAKFAST.

8 cups	assorted thickly sliced summer fruit with skin (use whatever is available: peaches, plums, apricots, nectarines), approximately 12 pieces of fruit
1 cup	blueberries
1 cup	raspberries
3 tablespoons	sugar
1½ pints	premium vanilla ice cream

Preheat the oven to 425°F.

Arrange the sliced fruit in a 12-inch gratin baking dish. Top with the berries and sprinkle with the sugar. Bake until the fruit is tender and berry juices are bubbling, 20 to 30 minutes.

Scoop ice cream into dessert bowls and spoon the fruit with some of its sauce over the top.

ALL ICE CREAMS (even premium brands) are not the same. Read the labels and check for gums and additives. The cleanest, purest, best-tasting products do not contain things like guar gum, carrageen, or locust bean gum. These are added to both thicken the ice cream and prevent crystallization, but unfortunately they taste just like they sound: gummy.

at blanchard's table at blanchard's table at blanchard's table at blanchard's table at blanchard's table at blanchard's table at blanchard's table at blanchard's table

198

Cracked Coconut

✳ SERVES 8

HERE'S A SHOWSTOPPER. IT'S AN ELABORATE RECIPE, BUT SO MUCH
FUN TO MAKE THAT IT'S WORTH THE TIME. YOU'LL NEED TO HAVE
SOME BALLOONS ON HAND—BUT THAT JUST GUARANTEES THE KIDS
WILL WANT TO HELP. SUBSTITUTE PURCHASED ICE CREAM FOR HOME-
MADE TO SAVE TIME.

16	small water balloons
12 ounces	semisweet chocolate
4 ounces	bittersweet chocolate
	Shredded coconut
1 quart	Homemade Coconut Ice Cream (page 201)
½ cup	Kahlúa Custard Sauce (page 211) or Chocolate Sauce (page 200)

Blow up the balloons to a 3-inch diameter. Line a sheet pan with parchment paper.

Place both chocolates in the top of a double boiler and melt over simmering water on a low heat, stirring occasionally. Remove from heat and let
cool slightly. (The balloons will pop if the chocolate is too hot.) Meanwhile,
place the coconut in a dry skillet over medium heat and toast until golden
brown, 3 to 4 minutes, stirring often.

Holding the balloons by the knot, dip them into the chocolate and roll
gently around until the chocolate covers the bottom third of each balloon.
Sprinkle the coconut onto the chocolate, covering it completely. Refrigerate or freeze for at least 30 minutes.

When the chocolate has hardened, pop the balloons with the point of
a knife, and quickly peel off the deflated balloons. Return the chocolate
bowls back to the refrigerator until ready to fill. Let the ice cream soften at
room temperature and spoon into half of the chocolate bowls, filling each
a little more than halfway. Place the filled "coconuts" into the freezer until
the ice cream is firm.

When ready to serve, scoop out a hole in the center of each about the
size of a golf ball. Position each filled "coconut" on a large plate and fill the
hole with Kahlúa Custard Sauce or Chocolate Sauce. Lean an empty shell
against each to make it look like it's just been cracked open.

Serve immediately.

at blanchard's table at blanchard's table at blanchard's table at blanchard's table at blanchard's table at blanchard's table at blanchard's table at blanchard's tabl

202

High-Tech, We're Not

MANY RESTAURANTS HAVE SERIOUS ice cream machines. At Blanchard's, we have a White Mountain Freezer 6-quart electric model. Clinton has tested many others over the years and after making only one batch of vanilla bean ice cream, he knew that this rather unsophisticated machine was the one for him. He handed us spoons and we all dipped into the tub for a taste. Clinton was right; the consistency was better than any.

The White Mountain Freezer has a wooden tub like the old-fashioned hand-crank variety and requires lots of rock salt and ice. It's simple but messy—too messy, in fact, to have in the kitchen. "No problem," Clinton said when we talked about the impracticality of such a machine in a commercial setting. "I just take it out under the tree."

Bob and I watched as Clinton set up for his ice cream production in the shade of a blossoming oleander outside the kitchen door. He arranged a small table under the tree, connected a long extension cord and motioned with his right arm as if to say, "There you go."

Warm Green Apples with Cinnamon and Ice Cream

WE LOVE APPLE PICKING IN VERMONT, BUT THE CHALLENGE IS WHAT TO DO WITH ALL THOSE CRATES OF APPLES. WE OFFER THIS RECIPE AS ONE SUGGESTION. (ALTHOUGH THESE APPLES ARE GREAT WITH CHOCO- LATE ICE CREAM, THEY'RE EQUALLY GOOD WITH VANILLA OR COFFEE.)

4	**Granny Smith apples**
3 tablespoons	**unsalted butter**
2 tablespoons (packed)	**light brown sugar**
¼ cup	**raisins**
1 teaspoon	**ground cinnamon**
1 pint	**chocolate ice cream**

Peel, core, and slice the apples ½ inch thick. Heat a medium sauté pan, melt the butter over a medium heat, and add the apples. Cook, stirring occasionally, until the apples are tender but still hold their shape, 10 to 12 minutes. Add the sugar, raisins, and cinnamon, and toss to blend. Serve warm over the ice cream.

t blanchard's table at blanchard's table at blanchard's table at blanchard's table at blanchard's table at blanchard's table at blanchard's table at blanchard's tabl

208

Mocha Fondue

✳ MAKES 2½ CUPS (ABOUT 6 SERVINGS)

FONDUE IS FUN AND MAKES A GREAT SURPRISE FOR DESSERT. IT'S "PARTICIPATORY FOOD," AS OUR SON JESSE CALLS IT. FONDUE GETS PEOPLE INTERACTING AND SHARING—AND WHAT COULD MAKE FOR A BETTER ENDING TO A DINNER PARTY THAN THAT?

SAUCE

1 pound	semisweet chocolate
¼ cup	strong brewed coffee
¼ cup	heavy cream
½ cup	Kahlúa

DIPPERS

FIGURE ABOUT ½ TO ¾ CUP PER PERSON OF ANY COMBINATION OF THE FOLLOWING.

Bananas, cut into 1-inch chunks
Whole strawberries
Orange sections
Pineapple, cut into 1-inch chunks
Pound cake, cut into 1-inch chunks
Starfruit, sliced ¼-inch thick

Put the chocolate, coffee, and cream in the top of a double boiler and heat gently, stirring occasionally, until the chocolate is melted. Whisk in the Kahlúa and remove from heat.

To serve, pour the sauce into small, individual bowls placed in the center of a dinner plate. Arrange the fruit and pound cake around the sauce and supply plenty of toothpicks for dipping. Alternatively, serve the sauce in one or two larger bowls, and place them in the center of the table for people to share.

sserts desserts desserts desserts desserts desserts desserts desserts desserts desserts desserts desserts desserts desserts desserts desserts desserts desserts dess

209

Kahlúa Colada

＊ SERVES 2

HERE'S A RICH AND CREAMY VARIATION OF THE CLASSIC PIÑA
COLADA. SERVE IT IN AN OVERSIZED BRANDY SNIFTER WITH A STRAW
CUT DOWN TO SIZE.

⅔ cup	**Kahlúa**
⅔ cup	**Coco Lopez cream of coconut**
2 tablespoons	**white rum**
3 cups	**crushed ice**
	Chocolate coffee beans, for garnish, optional

Combine the first four ingredients in a blender and blend at high speed
until smooth. If desired top each glass with a few chocolate coffee beans.

Chocolate Colada

＊ SERVES 2

THIS COLADA IS HALF DRINK AND HALF DESSERT.

¼ cup	**milk**
½ cup	**Coco Lopez cream of coconut**
3 tablespoons	**chocolate syrup**
¼ cup	**Mount Gay rum**
3 cups	**crushed ice**
	Grated chocolate, for garnish

Combine the first five ingredients in a blender and blend at high speed
until smooth. Pour into a highball or pilsner glass, and top with grated
chocolate.

PREVIOUS PAGE: RINSO

at blanchard's table at blanchard's table at blanchard's table at blanchard's table at blanchard's table at blanchard's table at blanchard's table at blanchard's tabl

216

Piña Colada

THIS CLASSIC, TROPICAL DRINK IS GUARANTEED TO TRANSPORT YOU
TO PARADISE. OUR VERSION USES FRESH PINEAPPLE INSTEAD OF THE
USUAL PINEAPPLE JUICE. IF THE PINEAPPLE IS RIPE, THE FLAVOR IS
UNBEATABLE.

⅔ cup	Coco Lopez cream of coconut
3 ounces (6 tablespoons)	white rum
2 cups	fresh ripe pineapple, cut into chunks
dash	fresh lime juice
3 cups	crushed ice
	Pineapple wedges, for garnish

Combine the first five ingredients in a blender and blend at high speed
until smooth. Serve in a tulip glass or pilsner glass, and garnish each with a
wedge of pineapple.

Mango Colada

✳ SERVES 2

FRESH MANGOES ARE READILY AVAILABLE IN SUPERMARKETS THESE
DAYS. JUST MAKE SURE TO LET THEM RIPEN FULLY BEFORE USING.
THE COLOR OF THIS TROPICAL DRINK IS JUST AS WONDERFUL AS THE
TASTE.

2 cups	very ripe mango, cut into cubes
3 ounces (6 tablespoons)	Coco Lopez cream of coconut
¼ cup	white rum
dash	fresh lime juice
2½ cups	crushed ice
	Mango wedges, for garnish

Combine the first five ingredients in a blender and blend at high speed
until smooth. Garnish each glass with a long wedge of mango.

inks drinks d

217

ndex ind

222

About the Authors

MARRIED FOR NEARLY THIRTY YEARS, Melinda and Robert Blanchard divide their time between Norwich, Vermont, where they built their own home, and Anguilla, where they operate Blanchard's Restaurant. They are the authors of *A Trip to the Beach*.